Archaeology Unearthed
Excavating Interest with Engaging Techniques

Table of Contents

Chapter 1. Introduction

Dive into the fascinating world of archaeology with us in our special report "Archaeology Unearthed: Excavating Interest with Engaging Techniques". Discover the nuanced art and science of unearthing the treasures of yesteryears, stories buried deep within the earth waiting to be told. This exciting journey offers a priceless insight into how gripping techniques and advanced technology are pushing the traditional boundaries of archaeology, converting intriguing uncertainties into thrilling certainties of human history and evolution. This absorbing special report is designed to spark your curiosity, whether you're a history enthusiast or a newbie adventurer. And believe us, by the time you're done flipping through its pages, you will find yourself gripped by the lure of our past like never before! So, why wait? Embark on this captivating journey and make the timeworn tales of bygone eras a vivifying part of your present!

Chapter 2. Excavation Techniques: The Heart of Archaeology

In the dynamic world of archaeology, where digging into the earth's layers is akin to journeying back in time, excavation techniques stand as the very heart of all operations. Every sweep of the brush, every careful scrape of the trowel has the chance to reveal groundbreaking insights into ancient civilizations or revolutionize existing understandings about the past.

2.1. Establishing the Excavation Site

The art of archaeology starts by the meticulous process of establishing an excavation site. Ancient pottery, tools, bones, ruins, or aerial scans of unusual structures are typical indicators of a potential site. Ground-penetrating radars often come in handy in non-invasively detecting these items or structures beneath the surface. Having identified a promising site, markers are set up to clearly define the boundaries, and a grid system is often laid out for strategic planning and documentation purposes.

2.2. Excavation Methods

Once the grid is drawn out and the site's pace is set, the digging begins in earnest. This process is a blend of art and science, of experience and intuition, of creativity and technique. There are two primary excavation methods in archaeological practice: vertical and horizontal.

+ Vertical Excavation Vertical excavation allows archaeologists to piece together the history of a site over time. It involves digging deep, narrow pits to expose the stratigraphy of the site - the different layers of soil representing different periods. This method is ideal for sites with a long, complex history, like the city of Troy, which revealed multiple civilizations stacked one on top of the other.

+ Horizontal Excavation Horizontal excavation involves removing one layer of soil across a large area before moving on to the next layer. This is ideal for exposing large structures or buildings, as used in sites like the Roman villa at Fishbourne.

Both methods require excavating in small, workable sections, or 'spits', to maintain control over the process and increase the chances of preserving artifacts.

2.3. Tools of the Trade

There are several types of tools that an archaeologist may use during an excavation, and these vary depending on the type and delicate nature of the materials expected to be found.

+ Trowels and Hand Picks The most common tools in an archaeologist's kit, trowels, and hand picks are used for clearing dirt and looser materials from artifacts.

+ Brushes and Wooden Spatulas When dealing with extremely delicate items like pottery, bone, or burnt material, archaeologists use soft brushes, often brushes and wooden spatulas, to clear around and expose them without damaging the artifacts.

+ Sieves Sieves come in handy to sort through the excavated soil and catch smaller finds like potsherds, seeds, or human remains that might have been missed in the first instance.

These tools, when wielded skillfully, help the archaeologist undertakes the careful process of 'digging' without damaging or disturbing the precious historical remnants hidden within the earth.

2.4. Recording Findings

Another critical aspect of excavation is the proper recording of artifacts and findings. This involves documenting the precise location, depth, and orientation of each find on a site's grid system. Detailed sketches, photographs, and three-dimensional models are also created to record the artifact and context in which it is found - this helps to build an understanding of how these historical pieces tie into a broader historical web. Our modern age also sees a fusion of technology with traditional techniques, such as the use of drones for aerial imagery and 3D scanning technologies to replicated artifacts digitally.

2.5. Post Excavation Analysis

Once all materials are unearthed and documented, the next stage is post-excavation analysis. This involves meticulously cleaning, preserving, cataloging, and analyzing the artifacts, employing a range of scientific techniques like radiocarbon dating, DNA analysis, and spectroscopy. As a science committed to reconstructing the past, archaeology does not end with the extraction of artifacts from the ground but ensues with studying these pieces to reconstruct our historical jigsaw puzzle.

Excavation lies at the heart of archaeology, but it is much more than just physically unearthing objects from the earth. It is a delicate dance of technique and intuition, a profound pursuit of knowledge, and an ongoing conversation with our past. It is an endeavor that requires discipline, patience, and respect, understanding that each scoop of earth moved, each object found, contributes to the canvas of human history.

Chapter 3. Piecing Together History: The Art of Artifact Analysis

Archaeological explorations—the process of uncovering the relics of the past—are impressive endeavors, but the work invested after these discoveries can be even more captivating. Post-discovery, the place for artifact analysis is where archaeologists seek to tell the tales of the past, through objects that are often silent, fragmented, or removed from their original context. By applying a variety of approaches and techniques, archaeologists reconstruct the narratives of ancient cultures, piecing together history in an engaging way.

3.1. Artifact Analysis: Core of Deciphering the Past

Artifact analysis is the interdisciplinary approach to interpreting the past, where archaeological finds are studied to extract valuable information about the cultures that created them. This process is often painstaking and meticulous, involving a thorough examination of each object's physical characteristics, including its form, material, and techniques used in its construction.

Let's take pottery shards, for example. By evaluating the material composition and style of each piece, archaeologists determine its age and the culture that likely produced it. The presence of decorations, their style, and symbolism carry narrative weight, offering glimpses into the society's values, beliefs, and technological prowess.

3.2. Material Analysis

The study of the materials artifacts are made from provides vital information about the knowledge and resources of the time. It uncovers ancient trade routes, technological developments, and resource availability, enhancing our understanding of the past.

For example, an analysis of bronze artifacts might reveal the presence of tin deposits nearby or burgeoning trade links. The style of the artifact could help identify which civilization it came from, even pinpointing influences from other cultures.

3.3. Contextual Analysis

Context is critical to the analysis of artifacts. Understanding the interconnection between artefacts and their location helps archaeologists draw precise deductions about the lifestyle, belief system, and societal structure of civilizations.

A ritual pot found in a residential area might indicate home-based rituals or important societal events, whereas in a temple, it would suggest religious practices. This kind of analysis cannot be drawn solely from the artifact but must consider its surroundings.

3.4. Technological Analysis

Analyzing the techniques used in the construction of an artifact offers insights into the technological capabilities of the civilization, their skill level, and potential cultural connections.

Analyzing the method of production of a stone tool, examining the knapping techniques, or understanding the pottery wheel's principles can help tell stories of human ingenuity and progress. This analysis is multidimensional, often encompassing visual examination, experimental archaeology, and even microscopic analysis.

3.5. Stylistic and Iconographic Analysis

Stylistic features, decorations, and iconography on artifacts are deliberate attempts of the manufacturer to communicate specific cultural ideas, beliefs, or simply their sense of aesthetics. They are potent tools for cross-cultural comparison and studying societal changes.

An artifact decorated with hunting scenes might suggest a hunting-based society, while religious symbols indicate belief systems. Shifting styles over time could suggest cultural change or external influences.

3.6. Interpretation and Writing History

Analysis inevitably leads to interpretation. A shift in pottery styles, the replacement of stone tools with bronze ones, the decline in building quality over time—all these give rise to a narrative, and that narrative is history.

Each artifact, however inconspicuous, carries a tale of its own. When examined holistically with other finds, they weave the tapestry of civilization's past, contributing to a clearer, fuller understanding of our shared human heritage.

Indeed, the archaeologist uses artifact analysis to cast light on the shadows of the past and to decipher the many stories that it holds. Each relic, each artifact, is treated as a vital piece of a grand puzzle, part of a collective endeavor to reconstruct the human journey through time. Pulling together these fragments, the archaeologist carefully curates a chorus of voices long silenced, transforming their whispers into scholarly discourse. This art—this science—is the very heart of artefact analysis.

And while the challenges are many, born from the complexities of interpretation and the elusiveness of context, the fruits of this meticulous labour resonate with the powerful effect: a deeper appreciation and understanding of our shared past, and in that recognition, a stronger connection to our common human experience.

Chapter 4. The Role of Technology in Modern Archaeology

Unless you happen to be Indiana Jones, archaeology, at first glance, seems to entail a lot of dust and hard physcial work. However, in reality, modern archaeology is a field that carefully interweaves technology and science, complicating the foundational fiction of an archaeologist with a shovel in hand. With the advent of modern techniques and the application of technologies from varying fields, today's artefact hunter is as likely to brandish a drone or a 3D imaging device as well as a trowel.

4.1. The boom in Non-Invasive Techniques

Recent years have seen a boom in non-invasive archaeological techniques. These contribute significantly to the archaeologist's toolkit, offering the means to scan and map archaeological sites, or even objects, in vivid detail without unearthing them. Drones fitted with photographic or scanning equipment can produce detailed aerial surveys of archaeological sites, revealing features and patterns that may not be discernible at ground level.

LiDAR, which stands for Light Detection Ranging, is one such tool that has revolutionized the way we understand our past. It uses pulsed lasers to measure distances and can often penetrate vegetation and forest cover to reveal hidden structures below. The use of LiDar in Honduras led to the discovery of a lost pre-Columbian city in the dense Mosquitia Rainforest, which was all but impenetrable before this technology.

Ground Penetrating Radar (GPR) is another non-invasive tool that uses radar pulses to image the subsurface. By sending electromagnetic signals into the ground and receiving the echoes bouncing back, archaeologists can create images of what lies beneath the surface, down to a considerable depth. This technology has been instrumental in discovering hidden burial sites and underground structures.

4.2. The Promise of High-Resolution Technology

High-resolution technologies have made it possible not only to find artefacts, but also to analyse them in great detail. New advancements in microscopy such as scanning electron microscopes and confocal laser scanning microscopy, allow archaeologists to study artefact surfaces at a nanoscopic scale. These techniques can illuminate the working, use-wear, and even the history of an artefact, revealing how it was used and by whom.

3D modeling and printing technologies, meanwhile, allow for replication of fragile or valuable artefacts. Using photogrammetry, multiple high-resolution images are taken from different angles and combined to build a detailed digital 3D model. This model can then be printed and examined by researchers everywhere, putting less stress on the original artefact and making worldwide collaboration easier.

4.3. The Age of The Digital and Computational Archaeology

Digital technology has significantly impacted data collection, storage, and analysis in modern archaeology. This digitalisation has enhanced accessibility, allowing researchers from different disciplines and geographical locations to interact, share findings and connect fragments of human history.

Deep learning and machine learning have been increasingly adopted in archaeology. Analysis software can now identify patterns and connections that may elude human researchers. Satellite and aerial imaging combined with machine learning can locate and identify archaeological sites, leaving archaeologists with the task of interpretation and excavation.

4.4. Advanced Dating Techniques

Technology has also enhanced the dating techniques available to modern archaeologists. Radiocarbon dating, which measures the breakdown of carbon-14 to determine the age of a specimen, revolutionized the field when it was initially developed in the 20th century. Today, advanced forms of radiocarbon dating, such as accelerator mass spectrometry (AMS), allow for smaller sample sizes, and faster, more accurate results.

Meanwhile, techniques like thermoluminescence and optically stimulated luminescence dating allow scientists to determine when an item last experienced heat or sunlight, further adding to the possible methods of accurately dating artefacts.

4.5. Challenges and Ethical Considerations

Despite these advancements, the incorporation of technology in archaeology has raised critical questions about ownership, access, ethics, and conservation. Issues such as the potential misuse of data, the oversimplification of complex archaeological findings and the over-reliance on technology pose distinct challenges.

In conclusion, technology plays an integral role in modern

archaeology, driving the field to evolve continuously. It is shaping archaeological practice, making it leaner, meaner, cleaner, and imminently more capable of deciphering the mysteries of the past. However, with all these advancements, it is essential to remember that technology is but a tool, and its efficacy and utility lie in the hands of those wielding it – the archaeologists.

Chapter 5. Geoarchaeology: Unearthing Landscapes of the Past

Reassessing our understanding of history involves more than just finding artifacts and structures. Geoarchaeology, an interdisciplinary field of study, demonstrates this by incorporating geological techniques into archaeological research. The exploration of landscapes, soils, and sediments ultimately enriches our comprehension of the human imprint on the earth.

5.1. The Scope of Geoarchaeology

Geoarchaeology employs a constructive blend of geoscience and archaeological methods to investigate the interplay between human societies and their environments over time. These investigations promote an understanding of human evolution, adaptation, and sustainability within varied ecosystems. The application of geological methods also aids in the systematic site investigation, identification, and subsequent preservation.

5.2. Interpreting Landscapes Through Time

Crucial to geoarchaeology is the understanding of stratigraphy - the layering of depositional materials over time. Stratigraphic analysis aids in the painting of robust historical pictures. Layers of soil, ash, rock, and other materials can yield important data about chronological sequences, changes in the environment, and the paleoclimate, providing context to the life of past societies.

5.3. The Significance of Soil

Soils reveal a rich tapestry of information about the past, such as the types of plants that populated an area, the animals that roamed, and even subtle clues into climate change. Palynology, the study of ancient pollen and other plant remains, helps document vegetative changes and human impact on the landscape. Ethnopedology explores indigenous knowledge about soils, which can yield valuable insight into past agricultural practices.

5.4. Human Response to Environmental Change

Geoarchaeologists explore patterns of human behavior in response to environmental changes. These patterns include migration, adaptation of processes, or shifts in societal norms and structures. For instance, the study of ancient sediments under the North Sea, known as Doggerland, illustrates how rising sea levels at the end of the last Ice Age led to a complete transformation of human habitation and culture in the region.

5.5. Sediments as Storytellers

Analysis of sediment layers can provide insight into human activity at archaeological sites. These sediments often hide evidence of past settlements, roads, and other features. By applying techniques such as magnetic susceptibility or X-ray fluorescence, geoarchaeologists can probe beneath the visible surface and learn about the environments in which ancient societies flourished or struggled.

5.6. Aiding Archaeological Excavations

An important aspect of geoarchaeology is in its potential to guide archaeological excavations. By providing preliminary landscape analysis and investigations, invaluable information can be gleaned regarding the most promising locations to dig. Additionally, after an excavation, a careful analysis of the stratigraphy can reveal critical information regarding the sequence and timing of human activities at that site.

5.7. Methodology in Geoarchaeology

The tools of geoarchaeologists continue to evolve alongside technology. Techniques such as ground-penetrating radar, remote sensing, and geographic information systems (GIS) are increasingly being used. These non-invasive techniques help in locating and mapping archaeological sites in highly detailed and accurate ways.

5.8. Climate and Archaeology

Climate change impacts are nothing new. Geoarchaeology delves into the archives of our planet to trace evidence of past climatic conditions and how societies adapted, migrated, or collapsed in response to changing climates. In doing so, valuable lessons can be garnered for today's society in the face of modern climate change.

Geoarchaeology is more than the study of ancient earth. It's a looking glass into the past and a compass pointing to potential futures. By unveiling the history of environmental changes and how humanity has adapted over the ages, it provides profound insights not just into our past, but also into future possibilities for resilience and adaptation in a changing world.

Chapter 6. Archaeological Dating Techniques: Understanding Timeframes

Archaeological dating techniques are observational tools that provide irreplaceable guides to the historical and evolutionary sequences of our past. Seen through the lens of technology and science, these techniques allow us to convert ancient remnants into reliable dates, aiding highly nuanced narratives to unfold.

6.1. Stratigraphy: An Introduction

Stratigraphy, a cornerstone of archaeological dating, deciphers chronological sequences using layers of soil or strata. The principle of superposition suggests that the lower layers are older, having formed before the overlying strata. The depth of the artifacts within these layers provides a rough age estimate, while soil analysis can further inform us regarding the conditions of the era.

Let's consider a table-styled examples, with fictional archaeological layers offering insights:

```
| Layer    | Contents                         |
Conclusive Information    |
|----------|---------------------------------
|---------------------------|
| Layer 1 | Modern artefacts                 | Present
to 20th century     |
| Layer 2 | Victorian-era items              | 1837-
1901                        |
| Layer 3 | Medieval tools                   | c. 5th-
15th century          |
```

```
| Layer 4 | Roman coins                  | 753 BC-
476 AD          |
| Layer 5 | Bronze age Implements        | c. 3200-
600 BC          |
| Layer 6 | Stone tools (Early Neolithic) | c.
10,200-4,500 BC      |
| Layer 7 | Palaeolithic Animal bones    | c. 2.5
million-10,000 BC   |
```

6.2. Radiometric Dating: Transcending Limitations

Although stratigraphy provides a basic framework, precision is often elusive. Radiometric dating, employing unstable isotopes, has revolutionizing accuracy. As isotopes decay at known rates (half-life), determining their remains allows us to calculate when the organism died.

For instance, let's explore Carbon-14 dating. Unlike stable Carbon-12, Carbon-14 decays over time. As living organisms consume carbon, a fixed C-14/C-12 ratio is maintained. But at death, the C-14 decays without renewed intake, altering the ratio. By comparing the present ratio with atmospheric levels at death, accurate death dates are produced.

Further, potassium-argon (K-Ar) dating examines volcanic rocks and ash adjoining fossil remains. Potassium-40 decays into stable argon-40, and given a half-life of around 1.3 billion years, K-Ar dating can date extraordinarily ancient remains.

Just remember that all radiometric methods have limitations, often necessitating collaboration of multiple techniques to circumscribe accurate timelines.

6.3. Dendrochronology: Unlocking Annual Secrets

Dendrochronology, or tree-ring dating, offers an annual precision that is simply unparalleled. Each year, trees grow a new ring; the thickness depends on the climatic conditions of that year. By analyzing this pattern, one can link it with a known chronology of ring patterns, offering precise dates.

=== Thermoluminescence Dating: Catching Echoes of Heat

Thermoluminescence dating, or TL dating, is used for material that has been heated, like pottery or burnt flint. When these items are heated, they release stored energy in the form of light. Measuring the light released, compared to the total energy stored, provides a date of when the material was last heated.

6.4. Relative Techniques: Positioning in History

Several relative techniques, albeit their lack of precision, sometimes offer the only lifelines to history. Techniques like artifact seriation depends on stylistic changes of artifacts over time. Cross-dating, while using dendrochronology principles, extrapolates dates from known sequences to unstudied regions.

As we delve into the annals of time with these dating techniques, it is inspiring to remember that science is ever-evolving. As techniques refine and new ones emerge, we edge closer to accurately tracing our labyrinthine human journey. Ultimately, each piece reclaimed from the past and diligently dated helps us assemble the vast mosaic of our collective narrative with growing clarity.

Chapter 7. Bioarchaeology: Interpreting Human Lives in History

Over the centuries, archaeologists have meticulously scraped away layers of earth and detritus, dedicated to uncovering memories of the long-lost human civilizations. However, among all segments of archaeology, bioarchaeology holds an undoubtedly unique place. By studying human remains, bioarchaeologists are able to bridge gaps in our understanding of the past and narrate tales of the trials and triumphs of individuals and societies through time.

7.1. The Bone Whisperers

Bioarchaeologists, often referred to as 'bone whisperers', analyze skeletal remains to provide insights into the life conditions of past societies, preserving historical narratives through the examination of human bones. These "whispers" from the past can take us on a journey into the lives of inhabitants of ancient civilizations, offering insights into health, disease, diet, violence, stress, and even societal structures and norms.

To gain these insights, bioarchaeologists utilize numerous techniques from multiple disciplines, such as biology, anthropology, geology and chemistry. Not only can they ascertain the sex, age, and height of the individual, but also identify any illnesses that they may have suffered from, or the physical labor they undertook — each bone acting as a historical document, holding fragments of invaluable information.

7.2. The Miracle of Osteobiography

One of the most fascinating techniques that bioarchaeologists use is osteobiography, a method that uncovers the life history of an individual via examinations of their skeletal remains. This involves looking at an individual's entire skeleton and identifying potential signs of disease, injury, diet, or lifestyle clues.

Starting from the skull down to the feet, each bone assists in piecing together the puzzle. Skull measurements can indicate possible brain development and capacity, while teeth provide clues about the diet and health. The study of spinal vertebrae can unveil manual labor history, and analysis of the hip bone may reveal the number of children a woman might have had. As such, an osteobiography can say a lot about ancient living and survival conditions, throwing light on social systems, nutritional health, and population trends.

7.3. Genetic Narratives: Ancient DNA

Bioarchaeology has been revolutionized by the advent of DNA analysis, an epoch-making event, heralding a new era of discovery. Extraction and sequencing of ancient DNA from skeletal remains has allowed scientists to trace genetic lineages, prehistoric migrations, and even inter-species mating events. It is giving us unprecedented access to the narrative of human evolution, each genetic marker stitching together an incredible story of our ancestry.

Our understanding of prehistoric migration patterns has become much clearer with studies indicating genetic similarities among diverse ancient civilizations. Furthermore, inter-species mating events, e.g., between Neanderthals and modern humans, have been unveiled through DNA analysis, transforming our understanding of the anthropological 'Tree of Life.'

7.4. Isotopes: The Chemical Diaries

Another significant advance in the field of bioarchaeology lies with isotope analysis, through which we can investigate ancient diets and migration patterns with increased precision. Isotopes of elements like carbon, nitrogen, and strontium found in bones can give substantial insights into a person's diet and geographical history respectively.

Carbon isotopic ratios can distinguish between marine and terrestrial diets, while nitrogen isotopes indicate levels of protein consumption. Strontium isotopes, on the other hand, are 'geochemical fingerprints', absorbed from the local environment and retained within the bones, providing a geographical signature. Thus, by providing information about alimentary habits and geographical displacement, isotopic analysis contributes significantly to the understanding of social and economic aspects of ancient civilizations.

7.5. Reading Disease: Paleopathology

Lastly, let's delve into another fascinating subset of bioarchaeology, paleopathology, which is the study of ancient patterns of disease and disorders. Skeletons of the diseased offer a snapshot into the histories of ailments that plagued our ancestors, helping us understand the factors surrounding disease emergence and prevalence.

Through the analysis of bone changes, human remains can narrate the stories of afflictions like leprosy, tuberculosis, syphilis, and arthritis, retelling tales of pandemics endured by the societies of old. Paleopathology thus enriches our picture of the past, offering glimpses into a world grappling with health and disease, and how they managed to survive and evolve despite adverse conditions.

Understanding these stories from our past forms the core of

bioarchaeology. It underscores our unceasing quest for knowledge, our resolve to connect with our roots, and our absolute unwillingness to let go of stories that have perished physically but continue to live on in spirit, within the bones left behind by individuals who once walked this earth. With every dig, every analysis, we not only unearth objects, but memories, narratives, wisdom and above all else, the resounding resilience of humankind.

Chapter 8. Maritime Archaeology: Exploring Underwater Relics

Immerse yourself in the depths of maritime archaeology, a specialized branch of this ancient study, that bears significant testimony to human seafaring activities over the millennia. By meticulously investigating underwater artefacts, sunken ships, inundated settlements, we can recover data that cast new light on our ancestors' maritime lifestyles, economies, trade routes, and battles.

8.1. Shaping the Course of History through Sunken Relics

As we delve underwater, we stumble upon countless ancient vessels, each holding invaluable knowledge from different eras. Sunken merchant ships, for instance, carry remnants of historical trading activities. They provide insights into the networks of economic exchanges that connected various ancient civilizations across continents and illustrate comprehensive patterns of commerce, culture, power, and politics. Similarly, warships give us fascinating clues about the evolution of naval warfare and the strategic importance of maritime routes in historical conflicts.

The invention of the Self-Contained Underwater Breathing Apparatus (SCUBA) post World War II was a seminal moment in maritime archaeology. While earlier, investigations were often limited to shallow waters and tidal zones, SCUBA facilitated deeper explorations into the seabed, unlocking a treasure trove of unexplored underwater heritage.

8.2. Intricacies of Underwater Recovery and Excavation

The process of underwater excavation differs substantially from land-based archaeology due to the unforgiving maritime environment. It involves rigorous steps of surveying, locating, excavating, and conserving the finds.

Before the excavation, a detailed survey of the sea floor is conducted using remotely operated vehicles (ROVs), sonar scanning, and magnetometers. This generates a map of the seabed with possible archaeological sites. The actual underwater excavation is painstakingly slow, often done by hand to ensure that no artefact or information is lost; water dredges and airlifts aid this process by removing sediment. The retrieval of artefacts is a delicate effort requiring divers to possess special skills lest they risk damaging these historical treasures.

Owing to the long-term exposure to water, sea salts, and microorganisms, the conservation of underwater artefacts is indispensable. Steps such as desalination, cleaning, and stabilization are executed before these artefacts find their way into museums.

8.3. Underwater Cities: Narrating Silent Stories

An archaeological marvel that seldom fails to arrest attention is the existence of submerged cities. Sunken due to natural disasters, geological phenomena, or rising sea levels, these ancient cities tell tales of civilizations long lost.

One such prime example is Egypt's Thonis-Heracleion. Once the pivotal port city of the mighty pharaohs, it plunged into the Mediterranean around 1,200 years ago, coming to light only in the

21st century. Thanks to the thorough archaeological investigations, we now know more about the city's strategic importance in international trade and religious activities during the Late Period (664-332 B.C).

8.4. Breath-taking Discoveries from the Abyss

Maritime archaeology has unveiled some of the most compelling finds that have enriched our understanding of human history.

The Mary Rose, king Henry VIII's favourite warship that sank during a battle in 1545, was rediscovered in 1971 and finally raised in 1982. The ship and her artefacts —from weapons, navigational tools to personal items— offer an unparalleled view into Tudor military life. Similarly, the Spanish Armada shipwreck, La Juliana, lost in 1588 and recovered in 2015, has shed light on the ill-fated expedition against England.

8.5. Charting the Future of Maritime Archaeology

As we move further into the 21st century, the advanced technology such as 3D mapping, photogrammetry, and satellite imagery is set to revolutionise maritime archaeology. These tools will not only support the study of complex underwater sites but also help safeguard our underwater cultural heritage against threats like looting and climate change-induced damage.

To conclude, maritime archaeology, an engaging offshoot of conventional archaeology, has profound potential not just to recount sea-bound stories from our past but also to reshape our understanding of how maritime activities have influenced the course of human civilization. As we continue to unearth secrets from the watery depths, we must strive to preserve these invaluable traces of our ancestry for future generations.

Chapter 9. Archaeological Ethics: Balancing Exploration and Preservation

The field of archaeology, as gallant and exciting as it may seem, is tied down by a series of responsibilities and ethical obligations. The treasure hunters of the past, unearthing artifacts without a second thought for the damage they might be causing, have given way to a new breed of cautious researchers and meticulous explorers. These stewards of culture believe in preserving the physical reminders of humanity's historical narrative, striking a balance between exploration and preservation.

9.1. Balancing Act: Exploration vs Preservation

Exploration and preservation can often seem at odds with each other. The act of unearthing artifacts invariably disturbs the site wherein they are found, often leading to its decay or destruction. Yet, these artifacts must be extracted to understand more about our past. Balancing these opposing forces is a challenge that archaeologists continuously grapple with and forms the bedrock of archaeological ethics.

9.2. Explorative Techniques and Preservation Needs

Over the years, refinement in archaeology practices has allowed us to extract significant amounts of information from sites with minimal damage. A great example of this is the use of non-invasive techniques for exploration such as Ground Penetrating Radar (GPR), Light

Detection and Ranging (LiDAR), and geophysical surveys. Such techniques provide crucial information about the site and allow the expert to make informed decisions about excavation.

With well thought-out methods, the need for massive trenches is replaced by smaller, more targeted digs preserving most of the site's integrity. In addition, digital technology offers the potential to capture, analyze and disseminate excavated artifacts and architecture without causing further damage or loss.

9.3. Responsible Collecting: An Ethical Obligation

The respect for the artifacts and the cultures they represent is a crucial part of archaeological ethics. Looting, trafficking and the illegal sale of artifacts undermines the ability to study and understand our past. It's incumbent upon archaeologists, museums, and collectors to ensure that their practices don't facilitate or condone these damaging actions.

Documentation is critical in this context ▯ artifacts are often most informative in their original context and relocation can sever ties to valuable associated data. Databases such as SITEARCHIVE allow for extensive documentation of each artifact's provenance and other relevant details, ensuring the value of the find isn't lost even when it's removed from its original context.

9.4. The Role of Local Communities and Descendant Voices

Inclusivity is another vital facet of archaeological ethics. One practical manifestation of this is considering and valifying the voices of local and indigenous communities. The history hidden in soil may be ancestral to these communities, and their interpretation of the finds can offer different perspectives which broaden our understanding of human history.

In addition, involving local communities can also be a way to preserve archaeological sites. By imparting the value of their heritage, communities engage in upkeep activities, preventing neglect, vandalism, and sometimes even proposing their land for archaeology, as seen in many Indigenous-led projects in Australia.

9.5. Conclusion

Archaeological ethics encapsulates a great deal more than protecting sites and artifacts. It's about respecting and preserving the often delicate balance existing between learning from these ancient treasures and maintaining their integrity for future generations. Embracing the local and indigenous voices in these pursuits can result in a more meaningful and multi-dimensional understanding of our collective past.

If archaeology is about unearthing stories, then archaeological ethics ensure that these stories remain accessible, evocative, and intact, despite the inexorable passage of time. In the end, our ability to fulfill this obligation will determine how well future generations will know their past.

Chapter 10. Public Archaeology: Engaging Communities and Education

Public archaeology, an emerging facet of the broader archaeological field, promotes engagement and encourages education of the public within the discipline. Stemming from a desire to make archaeology accessible and relatable to all, it focuses on the practice of including local communities, schools, and the public in archaeological work.

10.1. The Rise of Public Archaeology

It was in the latter half of the 20th century that the concept of public archaeology took root. Academics and practitioners alike began to recognize the need for a greater involvement of the non-professional populace in archaeological practice. This need was particularly propelled by two essential factors: the desire to enhance public understanding and appreciation for archaeology, and the escalating threat to archaeological resources due to rapid urbanization and looting.

It was now clear that the traditional approach of carrying out archaeology behind closed doors was not enough. Archaeologists had to reach out, open doors and invite public participation. The essence of the 'public' in public archaeology, thus, became about engagement and education.

10.2. Engaging Communities in Archaeology

Public archaeology seeks to engage communities by offering them a hands-on experience in the domain. The idea is to demystify the field, to let people know that archaeology is not about serendipitous discovery of treasure but about comprehensive, methodical exploration and study of materials to learn about human history and culture.

Numerous programs have been initiated to draw community involvement. Typically, these programs may include surface collection of artifacts, archaeological excavation under professional guidance, laboratory analysis of archaeological materials, and assisting in museum displays, to name a few. Through such programs, community members gain unique insights into archaeological practice, while they also contribute meaningfully to the research and preservation of their local heritage sites.

10.3. Archaeology and Education: Bridging the Gap

Accuracy of portrayal is another important aspect of making archaeological knowledge publicly accessible. Implementing archaeology in education has the potential to bridge the gap between public understanding and actual archaeological practice.

Educational programs aimed at different age groups have been designed to deliver accurate information about archaeology. Talks, workshops, exhibitions, site visits, and especially fieldwork opportunities have proven to be successful educational methods. Many institutions have introduced archaeology-based study modules and projects in their curriculum.

The goal is to not only offer factual knowledge, but to create an environment where students can understand the working methodology of archaeology, the thrill of the discovery process and learn to respect and preserve heritage.

Incorporating archaeology into education opens a window for students to explore the past, understand different cultures, develop scientific interrogation skills and instill a spirit of investigation.

10.4. Public Archaeology: Future Prospects

Public archaeology not only disseminates knowledge but can also alleviate some of the threats faced by archaeological resources. Education and engagement foster a sense of stewardship among members of the public, who become better informed about the importance of archaeological sites and artifacts and more likely to rally against their endangerment.

In a rapidly digitalizing world, opportunities to expand public archaeology are immense. From virtual reality tours of archaeological sites to online exhibitions of archaeological materials and open-access archaeological databases, the ways in which the public can interact with archaeology is more dynamic than ever.

As long as there is human curiosity about our origins and past, there will be an appetite for archaeology. Providing avenues for public engagement and education in this fascinating field will only serve to increase the appreciation for the stories etched in our history, waiting to be read. Public archaeology, perhaps, represents not just a new chapter in the discipline but an altogether new book waiting to be written.

Thus, through engaging techniques and innovative educational models, public archaeology creates a platform where everyone becomes part of the narrative of human history, promulgating the past into the present and the future. It is a journey that is, if anything, equally rewarding for the archaeologists and the public alike.

Chapter 11. The Future of Archaeology: New Techniques on the Horizon

Archaeology, as we know it, is a fascinating science of unearthing stories of civilizations that once thrived and faded into obscurity. However, the face of archaeology itself is in a phase of transformation as the industry is starting to embrace a range of advanced techniques and technologies. These changes could revolutionize the way we understand our past.

11.1. Geophysical Surveys

One of the most significant advancements in archaeology is the leap from traditional excavation methods to non-invasive technologies. Geophysical surveys are essentially tools used to map or model the subsurface without conducting an excavation. This imaging technology includes ground-penetrating radar (GPR), magnetometers, and resistivity meters that allow archaeologists to interpret what may lay hidden beneath the ground's surface.

GPR sends high-frequency radio waves into the ground, which bounce back when they encounter a buried object, providing an image of the hidden features. Magnetometers detect magnetic changes in the soil, which can indicate man-made features, while resistivity meters analyze soil resistance to electrical currents, helping identify hidden structures. These methods are not just valuable in mapping, but it also minimizes the invasiveness of exploring as many archaeological sites are also culturally or historically sensitive areas.

11.2. Digital Technologies and Databases

The proliferation of digital technology and data management systems heralds a significant shift in archaeological research and recording methodologies. Databases streamline documentation at dig sites and improve efficiency, allowing for rapid access to data and easy cross-referencing. Digital images, GPS measurements, and extensive metadata are meticulously compiled and stored, aiding in thorough analysis later on.

The state-of-the-art database allows digital data to be compiled and organized in a manner that can be quickly disseminated to scholars and the public. Digital 3D visualizations permit exploration of artifact details with microscopic precision, offering incredible insights into buried histories.

11.3. Lidar Technology

Light Detection and Ranging (Lidar) technology is another area where archaeology has taken a significant leap forward. This technology uses laser light to measure variable distances to the earth and creates high-resolution maps with minute details. It is particularly useful in regions with dense foliage where conventional methods might prove challenging. It's a remote sensing technology that enables archaeologists to map entire landscapes with remarkable precision.

Lidar has brought inaccessible locations within reach, enabling the discovery and exploration of intricate ancient civilizations. Perhaps its most significant contribution is seen in the discovery of the ancient city of Angkor Wat, where Lidar helped reveal the full extent of the complex civilization.

11.4. Environmental DNA Analysis

Environmental DNA (eDNA) analysis has opened up entirely new ways of understanding historical diets, diseases, and demographic changes. Extracting DNA from archaeological artifacts or soil samples from ancient settlements can reveal valuable data about the flora, fauna, and human inhabitants of those ancient sites.

This groundbreaking study helps to understand shifts in plant and animal species, human migration patterns, genetic mutations and diseases, and the impact of climate change on human civilizations. It's a kind of time machine, offering us a peek into our ancestors' diet, health, migration trends, and lifestyle habits.

11.5. Underwater Archaeology

With a lot of human history submerged underwater, the development of underwater archaeology techniques has been crucial. Advancements in scuba gear, sonar and photogrammetric technologies, underwater rovers, and improved methodologies for preserving artifacts under water have driven new discoveries from shipwreck sites to underwater ruins of ancient cities.

The application of remotely operated underwater vehicles (ROVs) and autonomous underwater vehicles (AUVs) has provided tools for deep-sea exploration without the risks and constraints linked to human divers. This has truly expanded the horizons of archaeological exploration.

With these advancements, it's clear that the future of archaeology is ripe with possibilities. While some might argue these technologies are distancing archaeologists from the thrill of physical excavation, it is unquestionable that they are opening up new opportunities for understanding our past. It is beyond a doubt that as technology evolves, so will archaeology, and such changes only promise to reveal more exciting secrets about our history and evolution.

www.ingramcontent.com/pod-product-compliance
Lightning Source LLC
LaVergne TN
LVHW010041070326
832903LV00071B/4735